# ENTREPRENEURIAL REVOLUTION

*Unleashing Entrepreneurial Revolution Through the Entrepreneurial Revolution Ecosystem*

By Emilio Cohen & Vlad Tseytkin

## *Table of* CONTENTS

Introduction ............................................................................. 3
Problem .................................................................................. 5
Analysis ................................................................................. 6
Eliminating the Root Cause ..................................................... 8
The Deal Structure .................................................................. 9
ER-ECO: The Entrepreneurial Revolution Ecosystem ............. 13
Technology ............................................................................ 20
The Original Case Study ........................................................ 24
Use Cases .............................................................................. 27
The Opportunity of the Century ............................................. 32

## INTRODUCTION

The business world has been shaped and reshaped many times over by government regulations.

The U.S. Securities and Exchange Commission has been entrusted with regulating the securities industry and enforcing the securities laws. These laws are powerfully restrictive and designed to tame entrepreneurial energy, tremendously diminishing growth and opportunity, as well as dramatically minimizing capital formation.

At the same time, these laws maintain the financial safety net. These very restrictions enable people to invest with relative safety and avoid devastating mistakes that are otherwise almost inevitable.

The underlying problems that the SEC is charged with solving are as follows.

1. A lack of reliable information about new opportunities, or even about an established company. The relevant information can be easily hidden or distorted, so a potential investor can't make a reliably informed decision.

2. A lack of experience, education, and professionalism possessed by the average unsophisticated investor.

3. Disproportionally high-risk investment opportunities.

The backbone of the existing system was built throughout the last century:

- The Securities Act of 1933 ensures that buyers receive complete and accurate information before they invest in securities. Primary equity markets are also regulated by this Act.

- The Securities Exchange Act of 1934 regulates secondary equity markets, which essentially means crippling the secondary market for the sake of protecting the public.

- The Investment Company Act of 1940 ensures that the public receives reliable information about investment companies.

- The Sarbanes–Oxley Act of 2002 targets maintaining the accuracy of financial information and the quality of auditing of companies by accounting firms.

It's important to realize that all the existing regulations don't fix the underlying problems. The problems are still there. The regulations only provide a certain minimal level of protection to individuals from the damaging effects of these problems.

This is where an opportunity presents itself. Imagine that the underlying problem disappears altogether and the multitudes of existing regulations largely become irrelevant.

Removing these powerful barriers will revolutionize the business world in general, and the financial world in particular. It's almost impossible to imagine what the world would become when the untamed entrepreneurial energy is allowed to flow freely.

This process is inevitable. It will happen sooner or later. However, even with the SEC and all its regulations in place, the impact of eliminating the underlying problem is still profound. Why?

Before we answer this question, let's consider the root cause of all the problems and the nature of the solution we're proposing.

# PROBLEM

The Howey Test is used to determine whether an instrument qualifies as an "investment contract" for the purposes of the Securities Act, and the definition is as follows: "... a contract, transaction or scheme whereby a person invests his money in a common enterprise and is led to expect profits solely from the efforts of the promoter or a third party."

In other words, the profits are to come solely from the efforts of others. If this test is satisfied, it is a SECURITY - a FINANCIAL INSTRUMENT, and it is immaterial whether the enterprise is speculative or non-speculative or whether there is a sale of property with or without intrinsic value.

The Howey Test is logically based on a much earlier observation by Adam Smith: the separation of ownership and control in a company might cause the manager to make decisions contrary to the best interests of shareholders.

The separation of ownership and control, being a source of great business power, presents the possibility of great danger to the shareholders. The consequences of this separation were carefully analyzed, understood, and regulated by the Securities and Exchange Commission. This very separation of ownership and control is what necessitates the creation of the financial instrument (i.e. holding shares of an enterprise through the financial instrument vs. direct ownership) and is the root cause of all the troubles.

Eliminating this root cause will effectively eliminate all the problems and dangers, as well as render the myriad regulations and many functions of the SEC simply irrelevant.

However, eliminating the root cause doesn't imply going back to a pre-separation business model. It means something else. To understand the proposed solution, we have to understand the root cause more deeply.

# ANALYSIS

Adam Smith observed and described the separation of ownership and control. However, his notion lacks precision, causing all the subsequent considerations to be similarly imprecise.

Namely, ownership and control can't be separated by definition. This is because ownership IS control.

The very concept of ownership needs to be redefined. Ownership is not binary – it's multi-dimensional. Ownership EQUALS control - literally. Owning something means being able to control that thing.

However, control has many aspects to it. Delegating some aspects of control to others, while keeping the remaining aspects of control means slicing it up, splitting ownership. In a way, this is co-ownership.

Let's look at what used to be perceived as separation of ownership and control:

The shareholders give over ALL aspects of control to the managers, except for:

- Once in a while voting on some matters, such as elections to the board of directors.
- The right to share in distributions of income.
- The right to purchase newly-issued shares.
- The right to the assets during a liquidation.

If you think about it, you'll realize that the managers are MUCH MORE owners than the shareholders, if such a comparison could even be meaningfully made. This is especially true in the case of minor shareholders, whose opinions are almost irrelevant even when it comes to elections.

The whole deal structure between shareholders and managers is intrinsically flawed and unfair. The "ownership" of the shareholders is so weak that they need serious protection indeed! Instead of separating ownership and control (which is impossible anyway, by definition), it's rather giving up the ownership and control, giving it over to the manager (CEO), while keeping only a faint shadow of ownership.

This is exactly why the SEC must interfere to prevent great damage that could be done, if not for the powerful restrictions which protect investors from damaging forces, while at the same time effectively shutting the doors to unimaginable growth and the ocean of opportunities that otherwise would become available.

The protection comes at an enormous cost, but it's well worth it.

However, it's only worth it until we eliminate the root cause by correcting the deal structure, which is something unheard of in the business world until now.

How can we do that?

# ELIMINATING THE ROOT CAUSE

The solution is stunningly simple. We distribute the aspects of control between the shareholders and the managers differently. More wisely. More fairly.

The idea itself is not new. It was arguably pioneered (in a different context) by Oliver Hart of Harvard University who was awarded the Nobel Prize in Economic Sciences in 2016.

Oliver Hart introduced the smarter allocation of decision rights as the remedy for the incomplete contracting approach. To oversimplify, the idea was that carefully allocated decision or control rights can effectively complete otherwise grossly incomplete contracts.

The flexibility of allocation of rights is crucial, because it should correspond to the perceived risk investors see in the venture, as well as the likelihood that investors will have to intervene.

Applying this idea to our situation, flexible and dynamic distribution of the aspects of control, carefully measured and balanced, powered by technologies that were unknown until very recently, make the solution possible. The root cause can be eliminated by achieving a nearly perfect deal structure, effectively protecting shareholders from uncertainties and contributing to cooperation to an unprecedented degree.

So, what is the perfect deal structure between shareholders and managers, how can it be accomplished, and how will the business world be impacted by this innovation EVEN BEFORE the SEC actually removes the powerful barriers?

# THE DEAL STRUCTURE

Shareholders and managers represent ONE WHOLE. Not including managers in the deal structure distorts reality, skyrockets investor risks, triggers potentially devastating consequences and is ultimately a root cause of all the securities regulations. The regulations help offset the negative consequences, but at a high cost: by taming and crippling entrepreneurial energy and not allowing economies to grow and achieve the highest level of wealth and prosperity.

This is the level we seek to impact. We "simply" correct the deal structure. Our deal structure includes founders, shareholders, AND managers. We then need to employ technology and tokenize this new deal structure (more about tokenization below). This will exponentially amplify cooperation, instead of amplifying problems, which is the case with tokenizing securities while underlying problems are in place.

On a practical level, there are 3 pillars to the new deal structure:

1. The Plan.
2. Board of directors.
3. Conflict resolution.

## 1. The Plan.

- The relationship between shareholders and managers is structured around The Plan. The CEO must submit The Plan, get it approved by the board members and execute it.
- When The Plan expires, a new plan must be introduced and approved.
- The CEO can't deviate from The Plan unless the changes are expressly approved by the board members.

- The Manager can't function without The Plan. All the company's activities are literally frozen without an approved Plan.

- How specific and how granular The Plan is reflects the trust the board members have in the CEO, as well as capabilities and experience of the CEO.
    - Full trust will result in carte blanche. In a way, it's a "paper" where CEO writes, "I will do anything I want," and the board members approve it.
    - Nearly-full trust will result in specifying a total budget to spend to reach the milestone, given the sought results; or, perhaps, a number of budgets, one per each suggested opportunity.
    - Limited trust will result in a more detailed, more granular, more explicit Plan.

- The Plan is a dynamic concept. It balances the relationship between "ownership" and "control," creating an amazingly efficient and effective deal structure.

- The CEO is legally bound by The Plan, but innovative technologies can be used to guarantee that the CEO won't be able to deviate from it. Or, more precisely, any deviation from The Plan must be submitted by the CEO and approved by the shareholders.

- What The Manager can or can't do is captured by The Plan, and is a reflection of the capabilities of The Manager, as well as how much trust the shareholders have in The Manager. The Plan allows a perfect balance.

- Needless to say, the top CEO - skilled, trusted, experienced, with a proven record of success - won't be limited by The Plan much, unless he or she decides to create a more detailed plan, even without being forced by the shareholders. The "better" the CEO is in the eyes of the shareholders, the less

detailed The Plan needs to be, the bigger allowed budgets are, the longer milestones, the longer duration of The Plan, etc.
- This new order is flexible, dynamic, balanced, and intrinsically fair to all.

There are generally four pillars to The Plan:

1. Milestones (may be based on dates, periods of time, money spent, activities and expenditures allowed or disallowed, etc.)
2. Financials (money, budget, dividends, etc.)
3. Ownership (shares-related, new shares issued, dilution of the current shareholders, buybacks, acquisitions, etc.)
4. Decision-making (decisions: initiating, approval, passing threshold; various actions, etc.)

## 2. The Board of Directors.

- By default, each shareholder is a board member. Yes, that's right: initially, all the shareholders ARE the board members.
- A shareholder, as a board member, has a choice: either to vote actively, i.e. to actually be a board member, OR to assign the voting power to another shareholder.
- A shareholder who assigns the voting power to somebody else is no longer an active board member, but at the same time can take the voting power back ANY time.
- The voting power of the board members is proportional to the shares owned.
- The company can also hire somebody "to sit on the board." However, this doesn't mean what this term used to mean elsewhere. This rather means that each shareholder has a chance to assign this new "member" to vote for them. Until assigned voting power by others, such a board member doesn't automatically have any voting weight.

- Some board members may become more influential than others. They may campaign. All the shareholders are given the stage to present their opinions and to demonstrate their expertise, to convince other shareholders to entrust the voting power to them.
- The board of directors becomes flexible and dynamic, powerful and effective.
- A shareholder can be as active and involved as he or she wants, or as passive and inactive as he or she wants.

## 3. Conflict resolution.

Conflicts are arbitrated as follows.

There are two steps in the process.

The first step:

We (the parties to the disagreement) determine if there is a person whom we both trust and we are ready to accept their decision wholeheartedly.

If there is such a person, let him or her "judge" the case.

Is there is no such a person, here is the second step:

I choose a person I trust; you choose a person you trust; our two representatives choose the third person whom they both trust.

Now all three people judge the case and the the majority decides.

So, who can be a judge?

Anybody, as long as chosen by the parties of the dispute, and agrees to assume the role of a judge.

A judge can agree or disagree to adjudicate any particular case. A judge may take a fee on a per-case basis, either naming the fee depending on anticipated level of effort or agreeing to the fee named by the parties to the disagreement. Both parties must pay the same amount to the judge(s); no party is allowed to pay more than the other.

# ER-ECO: THE ENTREPRENEURIAL REVOLUTION ECOSYSTEM

Let's consider an ideal ecosystem. It holds the five stages a company goes through, as well as capital markets where equity-based securities are traded and ownership of the company evolves.

There are five stages a company generally goes through:

1. The idea stage. An idea is born, brainstormed, researched, discussed, evaluated.
2. The formation stage. A legal entity is formed and registered, and the deal structure is crafted, fine-tuned, and finalized.
3. The fundraising stage. The company is funded. The shareholders acquire ownership.
4. The executive stage. The products or services are produced and delivered to the clients or customers.
5. The acquisition stage. Other companies are acquired, and the investment portfolio is formed and managed. (We won't cover this stage in this booklet.)

As far as capital market goes, there are two aspects:

1. Primary capital market.
2. Secondary capital market.

## The idea stage.

Where would you introduce and discuss new business ideas?

You could talk with friends, relatives, colleagues, social media platforms, interest groups, meetup groups, various events, work sharing spaces, startup accelerators, business incubators, or just fly to Silicon Valley and talk to everybody who walks by.

With many almost-obvious options and multitudes of players, there is currently no one obvious and easily accessible place specifically dedicated to the sharing and discussion of business ideas.

The opportunity lies in creating such a place. Bringing, validating and discussing your own business ideas, as well as participating in discussions initiated by others will be simple and easy, and, in a sense, irresistible. It will be filled with fun and purpose - to validate your idea for a startup, to catch great ideas of others in the earliest stages, to get feedback on your thoughts, to discuss and engage, or just as an entrepreneurial mental exercise - this is the Idea Part of the Entrepreneurial Revolution Ecosystem.

Once the idea is developed and validated, it's time to take it to the next stage.

## The formation stage.

There are many ways to register your company: from state government websites to multitudes of firms offering registration of legal entities.

But the registration per se is more of a commodity, and as such, it's not the main challenge. The main challenge is that sooner or later you'll need a law firm to get involved, because usually a long and complicated agreement needs to be drafted and signed. Moreover, the signed agreement will have to be changed more than once on the way, and this may create additional bumps - not counting time, energy, money and multiple pitfalls that need to be avoided.

The magic of the **Registration** (or **Formation**) **part** of the Entrepreneurial Revolution Ecosystem makes this challenge, as well as other registration-related and deal-structure-related challenges, irrelevant. Imagine the agreement being ridiculously short and simple, yet, more effective than any long and sophisticated custom agreement developed by the most reputable law firms.

Does this sound like science fiction? How is it possible?

- The theoretical answer lies in the incomplete contract theory and, specifically, in the contribution of Oliver Hart, which won the Nobel Prize in Economics in 2016.
- The practical answer lies in the new type of deal structure, outlined above.

The complexity and the length of current contracts is rooted in massive efforts to foresee the unforeseeable. Trying to predict and to manage anything that could possibly happen or not happen in future is the very culprit which necessitates complex and unfair contracts to be produced by armies of lawyers.

As Oliver Hart put it (in our words), instead of futile attempts to foresee and predict the unforeseeable and unpredictable, we should focus on distributing residual ownership rights wisely.

Practically speaking, in our case this means creation of two simple and effective devices: the decision-making device, and the conflict-resolution device. The need to foresee and predict details falls away, and so too the need to prolong and complicate the contracts.

This can't possibly work in a traditional enterprise for two reasons: an absence and impossibility of a simple and effective decision-making mechanism (as owners are forced to delegate their ownership to an agent - a CEO), and an absence and impossibility of a simple and effective conflict-resolution mechanism:

- Decision-making.
    - The "traditional" relationships between the shareholders, the board of directors, and the management are too convoluted. The shareholders own financial instruments instead of owning the company. The way shareholders

can influence decisions is awkward, too indirect and too inefficient to say the least.

- o The board of directors presumably controls the management, but in practice they have no choice but to delegate the full control to the CEO along with decision-making, and besides putting psychological pressure on the CEO, nothing can be done until the board recalls and replaces the CEO. This is a far cry from a simple and straightforward decision-making mechanism where an owner directly controls what is owned in a well-balanced manner.

- Conflict resolution:
  - o Conflict resolution is traditionally done via courts or arbitration. Legal battles in the courts are hardly a productive or even viable conflict resolution strategy. But arbitration, handled traditionally, has its problems: for example, lack of trust in an arbitrator or arbitrators, complications in enforcing the arbitration decision in case of non-compliance, complications with a choice of arbitrator(s), and availability and credentials of the chosen arbitrator(s), especially when dealing with long-term contracts or multi-national entities.

In the Entrepreneurial Revolution Ecosystem, these problems don't exist to begin with. Ownership of shareholders is restored, without crippling the creative energies of the CEO (in fact, the opposite is true: the CEO is empowered MORE by the higher degree of cooperation and support). Shareholders literally own the company, instead of owning the securities issued by the company, which enables an amazingly simple and effective decision-making device. The relationship between shareholders and management is perfectly balanced.

Our ideal ecosystem also provides a simple, practical, and effective conflict-resolution procedure (outlined above). This procedure is not new: it was practiced in Jewish law for thousands of years, yet for some inexplicable reasons was never borrowed by the legal systems of the rest of the world. Backed by the technology, it can take conflict resolution to an entirely new level.

With such revolutionary decision-making and conflict-resolution devices, the culture of long and complex contracts is rendered irrelevant. When you have such simple, effective, and satisfying ways to make decisions and resolve conflicts, there is absolutely no need to foresee the unforeseeable nor to predict the unpredictable. The intrinsically "incomplete" contracts become a source of strength instead of being a source of weakness, and, in a sense, are completed.

In addition to legal entity registration, both decision-making and conflict-resolution devices are implemented using the new type of deal structure in the **Registration part** of the Entrepreneurial Revolution Ecosystem, which corresponds to the formation stage of company development.

## The fundraising stage.

The fundraising process can be presented as a series of steps:

- Looking for potential investors.
- Screening.
  - The potential investors are screening the opportunity and the entrepreneur.
  - The entrepreneur is screening the potential investors who expressed interest.
- Socialization, nurturing, pitching.
- Diligence.
- Decision.
- Onboarding.

- Deal structure.
- Legalese.
- Signing agreement.
- Transferring money.
* Ongoing communication and the feedback loop.

The **Fundraising Part** of the Entrepreneurial Revolution Ecosystem takes care of all these functions and activities.

## The executive stage.

Well-developed technologies have drastically changed the way businesses are run. These days, it's not only unthinkable, but even unimaginable to run a business the way it was done a century ago. However, the heart of the matter - arguably the most important aspect - is still missing.

The services that have been available until now empower us to manage companies. They focus on management and execution. They don't facilitate or promote ownership of a company.

This manifests so strongly that in our corporate world there is no such thing as ownership! The shareholders are theoretically supposed to own the company, but they don't. They rather own the securities - the financial instruments issued by the company. We've mentioned this already, but we will mention it again. Because it's crucial. The difference is immense.

The Executive Part of the Entrepreneurial Revolution Ecosystem restores ownership to shareholders - something that has never existed from the times of the separation of ownership and control.

> The cornerstone of our business world and the source of our achievements, the separation of ownership and control, has been nevertheless critiqued since March 9th, 1776 (the date *The Wealth of Nations* was published) up till today. This is

because the separation created tension and animosity between ownership and control. It was noted, and for good reason, that the separation of ownership and control was a serious economic and social problem, which largely explained why corporations often did not act in the best interests of either their shareholders or the public.

The Entrepreneurial Revolution Ecosystem transforms the separation of ownership and control. Ownership and control are still separated, but differently: they now collaborate in harmony. This begins a new era in our society. The consequences are transformational for companies, and for society at large.

## Capital market.

We expect that over time the SEC will relax the regulations by such an extent that the shares of the companies won't be considered securities at all, which will make initial offerings of the companies on their fundraising stage, as well as secondary offerings immediately available to all.

Why are we confident that this is going to happen?

As we've already mentioned, the Howey Test determines whether an instrument qualifies as an "investment contract" for the purposes of the Securities Act. The shares of the companies hosted on The Entrepreneurial Revolution Ecosystem are passing the Howey Test with flying colors, which simply means that the shares in our ecosystem are NOT securities! The SEC will gradually recognize it fully, and in the meantime the recognition will be partial, gradually evolving.

# TECHNOLOGY

e are in the very beginning of the process of tokenizing the economy.

This means that instead of money and documents, we are going to deal with digital tokens.

How is a token different from money and documents?

1. More convenient and accessible.
2. Doesn't need cumbersome and restrictive systems (like banks, exchanges, teams of lawyers and accountants, etc.).
3. Enforcement mechanism becomes irrelevant (the technology facilitates automatic compliance).

On a large scale, one of the consequences of tokenization is explosive expansion of the relevant markets. Billions of people can now transact effortlessly. Trillions of dollars are now ready to be moved around freely, safely, and securely.

However, tokenization doesn't bring such an expansion in highly-regulated markets because the regulations restrict market expansion, even when other obstacles are removed by the technology behind tokenization.

One such example is equity. Tokenizing equity is one of the most rewarding and challenging phenomena:

- Rewarding, because it has the capacity to take cooperation and economic value creation to an entirely new level, leading to worldwide prosperity unprecedented in the history of humanity.
- Challenging, because equity is a security - a financial instrument. It's a subject to many regulations that restrict and

grossly limit the consequences and benefits of the new form of equity.

How has this challenge been solved until now?

On a superficial level - by trying to avoid securities regulations. For example, by registering a legal entity and conducting fundraising in Singapore, Switzerland, or the Cayman Islands. And then, if not defrauded, by implementing cumbersome processes that help avoid money laundering regulations and bring at least some of the money into the countries where investors actually live.

However, avoiding regulations, even when possible, is generally a bad solution: hundreds of millions dollars are lost without a remedy. Those who choose this kind of a "solution" simply forget that strict regulations exist for a compelling reason and are designed to protect our hard-earned money, as well as prevent actual money laundering.

Tokenizing equity doesn't solve the underlying problem. On the contrary, tokenizing the problem only amplifies the problem and results in negative consequences on a grand scale! Thankfully, our governments will fight these schemes more and more fiercely. A way of circumventing regulations is ultimately a lost battle.

We approach this problem on an entirely different level. We remove the root of the problem. Namely, instead of tokenizing equity, we suggest tokenizing deal structure - the new type of deal structure we've already described. In a way, this means tokenization of ownership itself.

A notion of equity generally implies a claim on profits and a certain deal among shareholders. Managers of the company have nothing to do with the deal. In a sense, shareholders are in their own "bubble," while managers are in their own "bubble." True, they interact once in a while through the board of directors, but overall they function independently.

Even though tokenization of equity can offer major convenience and, without a shadow of a doubt, facilitate growth, by itself it can't bring about a revolution. This is because we tokenize equity in a form of securities or financial instruments, which are subject to heavy regulations. The regulations restrict and grossly limit the consequences and benefits of the new form of equity.

This IS exactly the root of the problem. And this IS exactly what we're suggesting to solve by elimination.

Tokenized equity which is NOT considered a security will trigger The Entrepreneurial Revolution on grand scale. This is a "natural" continuation and the completion of the industrial revolution, but the achievements of the industrial revolution are a shadow in comparison with the consequences of The Entrepreneurial Revolution.

This is where our Entrepreneurial Revolution Ecosystem shines. As we've already explained, in the way it restructures the division of control between shareholders and managers; the shareholders end up as owners of the company, instead of being owners of securities the company issues. The shares in their possession will cease to be classified as securities. Yes, it will surely take some time for the SEC to acknowledge this fully, but at least partial recognition of this fact will be immediate, and it will inevitably extend and evolve.

This means that the ultimate impact of the Entrepreneurial Revolution Ecosystem is not tokenization of equity per se, even though this alone would be huge. It's rather tokenizing ownership itself. To be more precise, it's tokenizing ownership of value creation.

The distinction between equity (in its traditional sense) and ownership is critical. Yes, this difference has been overlooked for centuries, because it has been taken for granted that in the world of separation of ownership and control, a shareholder has no choice but to own a financial instrument issued by the company, which effectively cripples the ownership to such an extent that the arrangement shouldn't even be termed ownership.

Even tokenizing equity (in the sense of tokenizing securities) generates a huge impact, though to offset the dangers, the regulations must increase and become even more stringent.

In contrast, tokenizing ownership of value creation generates a revolutionary impact, at the same time eliminating the need for most of the existing regulations.

This changes the world. This is because economic performance generated by people **owning** the value creation will generate such wealth and prosperity that you won't recognize the society when this process evolves.

And if you wonder why this is so, the answer is really simple: this is what happens when unlimited cooperation in value creation becomes possible. Without The Entrepreneurial Revolution Ecosystem, cooperation in value creation has been grossly restricted and limited, even crippled, and real cooperation was not only impossible, it was unthinkable – partially due to a lack of available tools and technology, but more importantly, due to the lack of an appropriate conceptual framework.

# THE ORIGINAL CASE STUDY

The original case study which triggered keen awareness of the underlying issues and the first thoughts about the possibility of a solution was a company where one of the authors (Emilio) was a 10% shareholder.

The company invited an investor who purchased 75% of the company.

The CEO kept spending the money inefficiently, but neither Emilio nor other minor partners could influence the decisions of the CEO.

Why?

The main investor was too busy to get involved on a detailed level. All other investors resided in different countries and had no means of efficient communication between them.

Practically speaking, the CEO was given carte blanche and used it well. After burning through all the money, the CEO approached the main investor and asked for more money or the company would be shut down.

The main investor put more money in but made arrangement for conditions, trying to normalize the spending patterns.

However, it was hard to enforce. The CEO managed to transfer a million dollars to an account only he was controlling.

Without doubt, the CEO wasn't stealing. He did his best.

In the eyes of the minor shareholders who understood the situation very well, the CEO was very capable, but grossly inefficient and spent the money irresponsibly. But due to a lack of effective communication and a lack of transparency there was nothing they could do.

If they had full information, they may have been able to present the case to the main investor, and with that they would have had a chance to make him act more decisively, but they didn't.

The CEO didn't find it necessary to disclose all the information the minor shareholders needed to gather enough evidence needed to influence the main investor. Naturally, the CEO wasn't interested in getting audited, as this would be a distraction for him, while they weren't interested in taking him to court to enforce the information disclosure.

And what about the main investor?

The main investor was simply busy, as he had many other important things to do. Besides, he wasn't aware of the gravity of the situation.

So, what's the diagnosis? What was missing?

On the surface, transparency and honesty.

But deeper, it was about ownership. More specifically, the separation of ownership and control, which practically meant that the CEO had ALL control, including control over information (lack of transparency) and control over any money decision without having to justify anything unless questioned directly by the main investor (inviting a lack of honesty).

So, the real culprit was a faulty deal structure - an extremely inflexible and unfair distribution of control.

How would The Entrepreneurial Revolution Ecosystem make a difference?

First of all, it would provide efficient communication on the level of shareholders, management and projects, as well as across all levels. This would immediately take cooperation between all the players to the next level.

Second, it would ensure transparency. All the relevant information would be automatically available to the shareholders without them having to enforce their rights using the legal system. The inefficiencies could be easily exposed.

Third, the main investor would be able to limit the power of the CEO to begin with. He didn't want to give the CEO a carte blanche but saw no alternatives.

In real life, upon the additional investment request, the main investor attempted to limit the power of the CEO even though it meant time and effort spent with lawyers and plenty stress until everybody agreed and signed, but he couldn't supervise or enforce the new conditions effectively.

# USE CASES

## Case #1. Real estate agent.

A real estate agent finds a property which is well below market value. The agent may sign a letter of intent to buy the property, and even get the letter from the owner guaranteeing the sale for a certain price until a certain date. The agent registers the opportunity in The Entrepreneurial Revolution Ecosystem, with the appropriate documents and explanations, and raises the money from investors to purchase the property.

The agent acts as an entrepreneur managing the opportunity, according to the approved budget and the milestones, but the investors are watching over the progress and ultimately decide to hold or to sell, to renovate or not, to have the profit distributed among shareholders or reinvest it.

## Case #2. Real estate investment firm.

The firm buys and manages properties. Once on The Entrepreneurial Revolution Ecosystem, the firm can take communication and cooperation with its investors to a new level. This will enable them to find new investors much more easily and to keep existing investors much happier than they could otherwise. Here is why:

Investors can actively participate in decisions on whether to purchase certain properties or not, whether to sell other properties or not, whether to renovate or just wait, whether to get the profits back to the investors or use the money to invest in the new opportunities.

It's important to realize that active involvement of the investors in The Entrepreneurial Revolution Ecosystem is not a must. It's an option. It's an opportunity. They can be as active OR as passive as the want. And even if they choose to be passive, they can still assign a board member who they trust to actively participate for them.

## Case #3. A non-profit organization raising funds.

A non-profit is looking to raise money to buy a piece of property.

It's not easy to find donors willing to part with the money, even if for a good cause.

Once on The Entrepreneurial Revolution Ecosystem, a non-profit can offer donors ownership of a piece of the asset and optionally promise dividends. This could be accomplished simply and easily and would be much more attractive than just asking for a donation.

If in the future the property is sold, the donors would get their share of the profit; in case the nonprofit engages in commercial activities, as a part of their operation, the donors may receive dividends.

The Entrepreneurial Revolution Ecosystem offers non-profits a mechanism that can make them much more attractive to new donors as well as keep existing donors much happier. It's our vision that The Entrepreneurial Revolution Ecosystem will transform the world of nonprofits dramatically.

## Case #4. An office building (for example, WeWork).

A building with many offices rented out primarily to startups. There are many ideas and opportunities, both being born and developed here, hosted in the building.

The Entrepreneurial Revolution Ecosystem can enable cooperation between the startups - by grouping the startups in bundles. For example, the startups can partner up, investing in each other, dynamically restructuring the ownership to their benefit and raising funds at the same time. It should also be possible to invest in a bundle as a whole!

This would also be great for business incubators and accelerators, with ideas and opportunities "bundled" together around an incubator or an accelerator.

This would also work magic for Shark Tank, Dragons Den, The Profit, and the like, for both startups and established companies.

## Case #5. Elon Musk.

This is not about Elon Musk per se, but Elon Musk is just a perfect example, so we can't resist using his name.

- Elon Musk has MANY great ideas.
- Elon Musk has already earned great TRUST among the public.
- Elon Musk needs funding for his great ideas, and he needs funding quick!

What if Elon Musk could spend a few minutes describing the idea in The Entrepreneurial Revolution Ecosystem (in its Idea Part), giving it a few days to see if the idea catches fire and if yes, take another few minutes to register an entity and declare fundraising?

## Case #6. Public infrastructure.

The government works on many projects. Naturally, the government finds it very hard to find money to fund them. Railways, highways, bridges, airports, etc. Think about Dulles Transit Extension, Otay Mesa East, O'Hare Modernization, Crescent Corridor Expansion, Alaskan Way Viaduct and many others.

Once on The Entrepreneurial Revolution Ecosystem, the government can partner with the public, taking the cooperation to an unprecedented level unheard of in history. The government can make offers so much more attractive for people and companies to participate.

For example, the government can offer the public a share in profits, give the right to actively participate in certain decisions, and, of course, offer transparency which is a norm on The Entrepreneurial Revolution Ecosystem.

There are frequent calls for increased federal spending on infrastructure. This is a difficult conversation, given the inefficiencies and failures of past federal efforts. **Economists and policymakers are coming closer to the realization that the solution to America's infrastructure challenges is not greater federal intervention, but greater involvement of the private sector. This is exactly where The Entrepreneurial Revolution Ecosystem will shine**, providing a platform that can be immediately used for just that – dynamically and flexibly partnering public and private forces in a previously unimaginable cooperation.

This will bring the government and the people together. People will participate by investing and being actively involved in the infrastructure projects they believe in.

## Case #7. "One Belt, One Road."

China's initiative, "One Belt, One Road," promising more than **$1 trillion** in infrastructure and spanning more than 60 countries is a perfect candidate for The Entrepreneurial Revolution Ecosystem.

The Entrepreneurial Revolution Ecosystem would afford so many more people - including people in those countries the project is going to affect directly - the opportunity to invest in the infrastructure with transparency and trust.

## Case #8. A retail mall.

This may not be the most impressive example but it's important to realize that these kinds of opportunities multiply exponentially, and the ease of handling these opportunities, as well as efficiency, effectiveness, and transparency is staggering.

An owner of a shopping mall may want to become a shareholder of the stores that lease the space. The stores may want to become shareholders of the malls they are renting the space from.

## Case #9. Clients and customers as shareholders of a new type.

It's of great benefit for almost any company to convert their customers into shareholders. Not many thought of such a possibility, because it wasn't available anyway. With The Entrepreneurial Revolution Ecosystem, it's a reality.

A company loves its customers. The customers love the company they buy from. Isn't it a match made in heaven?

Even in pre-Ideal-Business-Ecosystem days, a company that doesn't learn from its clients and customers is guaranteed to fail.

Imagine the best clients and customers of the companies becoming their shareholders and directing and shaping the companies firsthand, instead of the marketing departments fruitlessly and painfully performing meaningless surveys and hiring behavioral psychologists to explain the behavior of the markets.

With The Entrepreneurial Revolution Ecosystem, converting clients and customers into shareholders will become a phenomenon, a mass movement, simply because such an arrangement is economically superior and astonishingly beneficial to ALL. Without a shadow of a doubt, there is nothing like investing in the company you buy from.

# THE OPPORTUNITY OF THE CENTURY

This is an opportunity of enormous proportions. It's bigger than the printing press, computers, and the internet. It's bigger than the industrial revolution.

For millennia, the world advanced slowly. There was hardly a noticeable difference in lifestyle from one generation to the next.

Today we live in a different world. Changes are frequent and dramatic. The world is advancing exponentially.

What is at the heart of exponential growth? What makes it possible?

Arguably, the best term that describes the heart of the matter is **"separation of ownership and control."**

Let's elaborate.

The biggest challenge to any progress and growth is a lack of capital. Great ideas, opportunities, and capabilities are plentiful, but without access to capital, an opportunity is dead. Capital is the fuel, the driving force behind any substantial development.

When ownership equals control, the vast majority of opportunities remain dead.

Why?

Because capital and opportunities don't come together. Because those with great ideas and capabilities rarely have capital to begin with. Because capital and opportunities don't meet, nothing is built, nothing is created, and nothing advances.

But it's more than that: when ownership equals control, most opportunities are not even born. This is because unless a person has capital, they normally won't bother exploring opportunities, as they know that they won't have continuation. So, most opportunities are not even explored, and most of those that are explored remain lifeless.

As ownership and control become separated, the capital markets develop, the oceans of capital are moving around, igniting current opportunities and inspiring so many new opportunities to be born. Separation of ownership and control bridges the gap between capital and opportunities.

This is the energy behind the industrial revolution. This is what propelled the drastic changes that brought about the advanced society we enjoy today.

However, separation of ownership and control has its disadvantages, and has been critiqued from the time of Adam Smith until today. It presents a serious economic and social problem, allowing corporations to act in ways that are neither in the best interests of their shareholders nor the public. Business corporations have been associated with excessive managerial power at the expense of stockholders, social irresponsibility, and internal inefficiency.

The benefits are overwhelming, so very well worth it, yet the disadvantages are many as well.

Governments mitigate the likely damages by creating multitudes of strict regulations. These regulations suppress the disadvantages to a certain degree, yet at a costly price: entrepreneurial energy is minimized and crippled.

We can't begin to imagine what the world will be like when capital formation becomes lightweight and accessible to all on both ends – the giving and receiving ends (i.e. for those with capital, and for those with opportunities) – if only the side effects of separation of ownership and control could be eliminated.

This is exactly what we've attempted to achieve. We've introduced the new type of relationship between ownership and control. This will trigger a next industrial revolution of grand proportions, exponentially bigger in comparison to the previous industrial revolution that created our modern society. We call this phenomenon The Entrepreneurial Revolution.

The Entrepreneurial Revolution is the ultimate completion of the industrial revolution. It's the industrial revolution the way it's meant to be. Restoring the perfect balance between ownership and control will have immense impact on the business world and on society.

The Entrepreneurial Revolution Ecosystem not only transforms existing businesses and propels startups, but also gives birth to so many new businesses that wouldn't be born otherwise.

- **The Entrepreneurial Revolution Ecosystem:**
    - **Helps companies and governments fund and grow their ventures more quickly and efficiently.**
    - **Establishes a new type of deal structure, inspired by studies that won the Nobel Prize in Economics in 2016.**
    - **Dramatically minimizes investor risk.**
    - **Takes cooperation and economic value creation to an entirely new level, leading to worldwide wealth and prosperity unprecedented in the history of humanity.**

For more information visit http://ereco.org

www.ingramcontent.com/pod-product-compliance
Lightning Source LLC
Chambersburg PA
CBHW030040230526
45472CB00002B/597